Anne Legge

AN AFTERNOON OF POCKET BILLIARDS

UNIVERSITY OF UTAH PRESS
101 UNIVERSITY SERVICES BLDG.
SALT LAKE CITY, UTAH 84112

AN
AFTERNOON
OF POCKET
BILLIARDS

Poems by Henry Taylor

Acknowledgment is gratefully made to the editors and publishers
of the following journals and anthologies, in the pages
of which these poems have previously appeared: *The American Oxonian,*
Appalachian Journal, Book Week, Café Solo, Calliope's Comments,
Cargoes, Carolina Quarterly, Cimarron Review (Board of Regents for
Oklahoma State University), *Contempora, The Daily*
Utah Chronicle, Encounter, Epos, Folio, Friends Journal,
The Hollins Alumnae Magazine, The Hollins Critic,
Messages (Little, Brown & Company, 1973), *The Michigan Quarterly Review,*
Mill Mountain Review, Monmouth Review, New Mexico Quarterly,
New Writing from Virginia (New Writing Associates, 1963),
The New York Quarterly, Noise Quarterly, Poems from Italy
(Thomas Y. Crowell Company, 1972), *Poetry Northwest,*
Poetry: Points of Departure (Winthrop Publishers, 1974),
Practical Horseman, Pucred, Roanoke Review, Shenandoah,
The Southern Review, Southern Poetry Review, Southern Writing in the
Sixties/Poetry (Louisiana State University Press, 1967),
Tennessee Poetry Journal, The Transatlantic Review,
The Virginia Quarterly Review, Wasatch Front,
and *The Western Humanities Review.*

"Bernard and Sarah," "Breakings," "Buildings and Grounds,"
"Burning a Horse," "Campaign Promise," "Riding Lesson," and "Speech"
were published in 1971 in *Breakings,* a limited edition produced by
The Solo Press, San Luis Obispo, California.

Lines from "No Man's Good Bull" from the book
Let Not Your Hart, copyright © 1968 by James Seay. Reprinted by
permission of the author and Wesleyan University Press.

Lines from "Ecloga III" from the book *The Eclogues and the Georgics of*
Virgil, copyright © 1971, 1972 by David R. Slavitt. Reprinted by
permission of the author and Doubleday & Company.

English translation of the poetry of Giuseppe Ungaretti
published with the permission of Cornell University Press.

And so no force, however great, can stretch
a cord, however fine, into a horizontal line
which shall be absolutely straight.

William Whewell
Elementary Treatise on Mechanics (1819)

For
George Garrett, Louis Rubin,
William Jay Smith, and
Tom Taylor,
old artificers

The Poems

I BREAKINGS

II LEARNING TO FACE EXTINCTION

III *FROM PORLOCK*

IV *HARVEST*

I *Breakings*

Breakings

Long before I first left home, my father
tried to teach me horses, land, and sky,
to show me how his kind of work was done.
I studied how to be my father's son,
but all I learned was, when the wicked die,
they ride combines through barley forever.

Every summer I hated my father
as I drove hot horses through dusty grass;
and so I broke with him, and left the farm
for other work, where unfamiliar weather
broke on my head an unexpected storm
and things I had not studied came to pass.

So nothing changes, nothing stays the same,
and I have returned from a broken home
alone, to ask for a job breaking horses.
I watch a colt on a long line making
tracks in dust, and think of the kinds of breakings
there are, and the kinds of restraining forces.

Because of a promise I cannot break
I have returned to my father's house, and here,
for the first time in years, I have risen
early this Sunday to visit the Friends.
As I drive to the Meeting House, the trees
wave softly as the wind moves over me.

I am late. Faces turn to look at me;
I sit in a pew apart, and silence breaks
slightly, like the rustle of old trees.
I wonder whether I am welcome here,
but in the old wall clock I see a friend.
An old man I remember now has risen

to say that this is Easter. Christ has risen.
The ticking of the old wall clock distracts me
as this old man addresses his friends;
he prowls for an hour through a Bible, breaks
his voice to bring my wandering mind back here
from aimless circling through the aging trees

whose branches tick like clocks. Boughs cut from trees,
disposed through the room, remind me of the risen
Christ this voice speaks of; I do not see him here.
I do not see him here, but flowers tell me,
on the mantel before us, in scent that breaks
above the graying heads of nodding Friends,

on hats and in lapels of aging Friends,
the flowers and the branches from the trees
remind me of what this old man's voice breaks
for the last time to tell us: Christ has risen.
With the tongue of a man he speaks to me
and to his Friends: there are no angels here.

Goodbye
to the
Old Friends

4

At last I shout without breath my first prayer here
and ask for nothing but silence. Two old Friends
turn slowly toward each other, letting me
know how much silence remains. The trees
ripple the silence, and the spirit has risen.
Two old hands of marble meet and Meeting breaks.

Old Friends move over the lawn, among old trees.
One offers me his hand. I have risen,
I am thinking, as I break away from here.

Girl with a Flute

for Ann Cherry

She appeared, and there were no
words spoken. She stood with
her back and her long blond
hair to the wall, as,

in the days of heroes,
stone women by the score
held on their patient heads
the roofs of Grecian temples.

Time goes by, and on
those isles, the wind has blown
their stone clothes thin; but now,
upon a sign ceremoniously

given, she sits with her
wide skirt around her, takes
up with care the silver
flute, and moves as no one

ever has, and makes such sounds
as men, as men are now,
have never heard before.
The music stops; she bows,

walks to the door and rises
slowly, smiling, through the air,
playing the Haydn Flute Concerto
as she rides the wind away.

You ask me if I think you do not care
And I shall say some words to the receiver
And fear they will not be the words you hear:
I cannot lay my hand upon your shoulder.

Long
Distance

*December
Love Song*

Outside the diner, snow
    muffles the lighted street.
You sit before me now,
and I, through smoke and steam,
    stare at your lips, repeat
not yours, but words I dream
        you send above the chink
        of forks and plates. I shrink,

become a boy of eight
    perched on a washing machine:
close to our inadequate
and antiquated radio,
    I dream my ears as keen
as those of stern-lipped Tonto
        warning the Lone Ranger
        of imperceptible danger.

All my childish wishes
    concentrate on static,
the clatter of the dishes
in the sink before my mother,
    the roar of the automatic
washing machine, all other
        disruptive sounds that can
        drown out the tall Masked Man

and the Indian, the sounds
    from good and bad guys' guns.
My heart is out of bounds
now, beyond the swinging door,
    beyond the cinnamon buns
untouched on the plate before
        your eyes that try to reach
        beyond attempts at speech,

back with the drum of hooves,
     the note of recognition —
as the White Horse Silver moves
across the plain, following
     the wind and the donation
of the Bullet — in the bellowing
     of one proud man who knows
     the Masked Man and tells those

who wondered who this was
     whose ringing voice is dying
now. Outside, the snow is
falling on the street, on eyes,
     the White Horse Silver, lying
on lips, your voice that tries
     to reach across this table, where
     it dies, drowned out in static air.

Goodbye
to the
Goya Girl

*Woman with
a Scarf*

When we were formally introduced
I was expected to doubt
that you could speak through that glass.
She had no reason to suspect
that you were the best of backbiters.

The way you used that glass was like a woman,
holding it so carefully between us,
the finishing touch to your face.

I fell for your eyes and mouth, your voice
most of all. I wanted even those arms
around me, and they were.

He travels fastest who travels alone,
And he kills two birds with one rolling stone.

Divorce

Among the Departures from This House

In Coke bottles waiting to be returned,
under the faded couch, beside the bed,
in empty cups which perch about the room,

dust settles, gathers, breeds, and comes alive.
It grows like snow — nothing improves before
the slow and tactless onslaught of my hands,

until, as I lie sifting toward sleep,
the little balls of dust unite, fall in,
move out like lemmings, marching against the wind.

An Afternoon of Pocket Billiards

Here where there is neither hope nor haste
all my days blend; each dark day is misplaced
        inside my crowded head.
I try to beat a game, half chance, half cold
and steady practice, struggling for the skill
that might kill chance. But chance's claws take hold,
the game is wrecked, and time is all I kill:
no sleight of hand or heart can overcome
the fear that, in this darkness, only time
        is not already dead.

I narrow down my gaze to where I waste
days growing used to a dusty taste
        that hangs in the dead air;
motes of chalk and talcum powder sift
down past the hard edge of the swinging light
above my table. Jukebox voices drift
by me through the dark, raveled with a slight
vibration from that older world beyond
the window: now I listen for a sound
        that may still rise somewhere

        this afternoon, away
from here . . . my eyes wander from where I play
to the motions of more skillful hands than mine:
another player leans above his cue.
Between us, those old tremors seem to move
the air I stare through, almost as if you
were breathing here: that half-remembered love
        obscures the perfect shot
I turned to watch; I turn back, but am caught
between my past and the shifting design

on a green field of order where I wait
for time and strength of will to dissipate
      these shapes that coil and turn
above the hush and click of herded spheres.
Brief glimpses of a chain of treacheries
flicker around a melody that bears
into this room the gradual disease
we fled when you tore blindly out our driveway
for the last time, and I came here to play,
      to wait for your return,

for this game's random shifts to bring you back
or set me free. As I blunder through each rack,
      no two shots are the same;
yet if, beneath them all, dim certainties
evolve to hold my called shots on a course
that weaves beyond love's sudden vagaries,
still, an impulse like love, in the force
behind that wavering song, caroms my thought
into an old mistake: with every shot
      I call, I speak your name.

High and low, striped and solid balls rotate
in endless formations as time grows late.
      My concentration breaks
just at the dead-reckoned instant before
each shot: testing stroke and angle, I ease
down on the felt and line it up once more;
too late, I feel that slight vibration seize
my arm — too late to stand. My knocking heart
shatters skill and chance, and takes the game apart.
      I make my own mistakes.

I chalk my cue and call for one more rack,
believing I might still untwist the wreck
              your song makes in my head.
I think how spellbound Bottom woke to shout
through nightmare trees, "When my cue comes, call me,
and I will answer . . ." Your voice might find me out,
note by note unraveling to recall me
from this enchanted wood beyond your reach.
"When my cue comes . . ." Moving only by touch,
              I try to hold the thread,

listening for the words to an old song
that draws me down, sets me adrift among
              patterns below the game.
The words will not connect. Red blood and bone,
older than love, the swirling echo drives
me down below green felt toward solid stone
whose grains read out the sequence of my lives
in sounds like underwater footsteps. My blind
and whispering fingers stroke the stone to find
              strength to forget the shame

I learned too long ago. I may be wrong
to follow an ancient, dimly-sounding song
              whose melody is fear,
whose words might never speak; but now I know
that in it, somewhere, forces of hand and will
combine like dancers on a stage. And now,
within the strictness of my touch, I feel
a surge of steadiness. I rise to air,
to dust and vacant noise and old despair.
              Error still holds me here,

but I'll be right someday:
though one song of old love has died away,
an older song is falling into place.
From now on I will play to make it speak,
to see the form its words give to this game.
I see, as I move into another rack,
that all days in this cavern are the same:
        endless struggles to know
how cold skill and a force like love can flow
together in my veins, and be at peace.

Here where there is neither hope nor haste
I narrow down my gaze to where I waste
        this afternoon away;
on a green field of order, where I wait
for this game's random shifts to bring you back,
high and low, striped and solid balls rotate.
I chalk my cue and call for one more rack,
listening for the words to an old song
I learned too long ago: "I may be wrong,
        but I'll be right someday."

The hills where I grew up had learned to hide
destructions from each other long before
Hughesville saw destruction take its store,
and still the Hughesville legend has not died:

The Hughesville Scythe

how once the storekeeper unlocked the door
to find he had been robbed. One clue, beside
the hearth, a swallow's nest on the stone floor,
told him how the burglar had got inside.

The old man took a scythe-blade from his store
and fixed it in the chimney, across the fine-
edged dark, where it would split a man who tried
to come that way again and steal his gold.

No burglar ever came. Now those designs
are choked in honeysuckle, and the old
insistent rituals of decay unfold;
yet in my brain that unused blade still shines,

and when I try to walk through dark I hold
my hand before me, touching solid signs,
thinking how a man can seek for gold
and lie in pieces in the raging vines.

II *Learning To Face Extinction*

Pastoral

for
David R. Slavitt

In the country, you learn to live at peace
with your neighbor; he is farther away,
but when you meet, you always stop and talk.

You learn that he is a pathologist
who every day kisses his wife goodbye
and goes to the lab, and blows up a goat.

The trees grow up around you as he speaks.

Afterwards, he counts the fragments, notes
their average size, and calculates the impact
with which they struck the walls.
                                    In the evening,
you might hear him mowing his lawn, or closing
his garage door for the night. Cricket sounds
surround you both out here; in the morning,
when you pass him on the road, you smile and wave.

21

Amazing but True

In the Chamber of Natural Curiosities,
a man cries "Fraud!" and points
at the two-headed calf, his finger tracing
what might be the seam of the taxidermist's needle
around the base of one head's neck.

One way or the other, craft or miraculous birth,
it has found its way here
to this fly-specked wood shelf. Its four plastic eyes
stare a message you can never forget: born or made,
it is something you have to believe.

Snapshot

So huge he couldn't reach below his belt
(he'd been a sideshow fat man for a while),
Mr. Shipman always kept a boy with him
whose job, whenever he was called upon,
was to unbutton that enormous fly,
reach in and grab, then stand aside and aim.
Once, behind the grandstand at a ball game,
while Shipman shifted his impatient flesh
from foot to foot, the boy groped in the trousers
and said, "Mr. Shipman, I can't find it." "Well,
God damn it, boy, you the last man had it."

*Riding
Lesson*

I learned two things
from an early riding teacher.
He held a nervous filly
in one hand and gestured
with the other, saying, "Listen.
Keep one leg on one side,
the other leg on the other side,
and your mind in the middle."

He turned and mounted.
She took two steps, then left
The ground, I thought for good.
But she came down hard, humped
her back, swallowed her neck,
and threw her rider as you'd
throw a rock. He rose, brushed
his pants and caught his breath,
and said, "See, that's the way
to do it. When you see
they're gonna throw you, get off."

*Campaign
Promise*

During the Great Debates, he tried a joke
and nothing happened. For an instant, hatred
for everything he saw leapt from his eyes
to his mouth, and down his arm to one hand
the camera caught and held as it gripped something —
the lectern, a table's corner, I forget what —
which, had it been alive, he would have killed.

How It Looks on Paper

for Jack Vernon

The President's hands rove
lovingly over a sheet of paper.

And right here under this tree,

As usual, here's Vietnam. That's
the Delta, of course, and

his damp foot touching real soil,

over here, this crosshatched
area, we have Cambodia. Now

his small ear straining for something

these small black regions here,
these kidney-shaped spots

that even in this place sounds wrong,

on the border, these are pockets
of resistance (see illustration).

wondering what is about to emerge

If some of the men stationed
in this white part of the page

from the heavy fog rolling toward him,

are moved across here into this
crosshatched sector, then we can

a boy with dark eyes waits to see

26

make a quick sweep, like
this, and eradicate a serious

    whether his luck will hold out,

threat to the many American
lives now occupying this

    and if so, where it will take him.

portion of the page, down here.

Speech

1

I crouch over my radio
to tune in the President,
thinking how lucky I am
not to own a television.

2

Now the rich, cultivated voice
with its cautious, measured pauses
fills my living room, fills
the wastebasket, the vase
on the mantel, the hurricane
lamps, and even fills
the antique pottery whiskey jug
beside the fireplace, nourishing
the dried flowers I have put in it.

3

"I had a responsibility,"
he says; the phrase pours
from the speaker like molasses,
flows to the rug, spreads
into a black, shining puddle,
slowly expands, covers
the rug with dark sweetness.
It begins to draw flies;
they eat all the syrup
and clamor for more.

4

I can barely hear the speech
above the buzzing of their wings.
But the Commander in Chief
has the solution: another
phrase, sweeter, thicker,
blacker, oozes out

over my living room floor:
"I have personal reasons
for wanting peace." This is more
than the flies will be able to eat;
they will stay quiet
for the rest of the speech.

5

Now, you are thinking, comes
the Good Part, the part
where the syrup proves poisonous
and kills all the flies.
My fellow Americans, that
is not at all what happened.
The flies grew fat on the phrases,
grew as large as bullfrogs.

6

They are everywhere in the house,
and the syrup continues
to feed and fatten them;
in the pottery whiskey jug,
sprouting new leaves and buds,
even the dried flowers thrive.

7

The speech
has been over for weeks now;
they go on eating,
but they stay quiet
and seem peaceful enough.
At night, sometimes,
I can hear them
making soft liquid sounds
of contentment.

Toad

Squat in the stagnant sunlight
on the moss beneath a shrub
its tongue slowly flicking
its throat slowly throbbing
huddled alone in the wood.
A ten-year-old boy exploring
found it damp and sparkling there
and caught it up in his hands.
He felt the frightened
water on his fingers.
Into his pocket carefully
so he could carry it home
and down on the floor he played
making it hop for his joy.
But the room was too dry
it heaved for air and died
dust clinging to its skin.
Weeping he knelt on the floor
holding this love in his fingers
waiting for someone to speak.
Before he went to bed
he put it in a box
and hid it in his closet
behind a baseball glove.

STORM MOUNTAIN SLIDE AREA

I stop my car on a curve in a canyon road,
between two signs forbidding my parking here.
Above my head uncountable tons of snow
hover precariously on the mountainside.

Below me and to the west, the yellow dome
of Salt Lake City's man-made atmosphere
undulates against the upper air.
Farther up, to the east, the Rangers' cannon
topples the wavering balance on another hill.

Above my head a mountain is holding its breath.

SALT STORM

All day high winds swept in from the west,
lifting alkali and salt toward the sky,
blotting out the sun, turning the valley gray.
At nightfall, a light rain brought all down.

This morning, people stand beside their cars
in long lines at the automatic car wash,
testing their smudged fingers on their tongues.

One by one, they ease into the dark
tunnel of nozzles and steam; the fine spray
clouds and hits the gutters toward the storm drains.

Water-beaded cars nose out into the streets,
roaring into the first clear day this spring.

*Learning
To Face
Extinction*

THE VIEW FROM A CAB

An odd day. For the first time in years,
I am in New York. Riding in from
the airport on the bus, I have seen
abandoned cars spilling out their guts
onto loops of freeway cloverleaves.
The light looks dangerous. Anywhere else,
people would expect a hurricane:
the haze on the city has an edge,
like an inverted saucer. The sun
pries up one edge with a slanting ray.
I get in a cab. "This weather, huh?
I tell you what, it's them astronauts,
they're the cause of it." "How's that?" I say.
"I'm not sure," he says, "but I know this:
fuck with the moon, the sun don't like it."

Buildings
and Grounds

for
Richard Dillard

The house we moved into has been landscaped
so that it has the portable, plastic look
of a Sears, Roebuck toy farm.

All up and down our street, the same minor artist seems
to have been at work; our neighbors' lawns are
watered and mowed truly until they are carpets,

their shrubs are lovingly trimmed and shaped
into green velvet eggs and spheres.
Our neighbors watch us like hawks,

wondering whether we have the equipment,
the know-how, the spirit, to strive with them
as they strive with their landscapes.

Oh, let me bring my home from the South to this street!
I will let the grass grow until it is knee-high,

I will import chickens and a blue-tick hound to trample
the grass and dig bone-holes and scratch-holes,

I will set up on cinderblocks in the front yard
a '38 Ford with no tires or headlights,
to shelter the hound and the chickens,

I will sit in the gutted driver's seat
with a bottle of Old Mr. Mac, glaring at my
neighbors, reading aloud from *God's Little Acre*,

I will be a prophet of wildness and sloth!

But the Puritan gaze of my neighbors cuts through
my desperate vision of home — my dream house
will not flourish here.

I will spend my rapidly declining years
          reading the labels on bags of crabgrass killer,

pushing my lawn mower until my front yard
          is as smooth as a green on a golf course,

clipping and shaping my landlord's opulent shrubs.

But don't misunderstand me — I have not been
          converted; I will still make something
          to sustain me here in this alien land.

I will plant mint in the flowerbeds beside
          the Shasta daisies we brought from Monticello,

I will set up a croquet course on the front lawn
          with a slender drink-stand at each wicket
          to hold my frosty mint juleps,

I will station an iron jockey by the driveway
          to stare back into the pitiless eyes
          of my neighbors' pink plastic flamingoes,

I will keep a Tennessee Walking Horse in the garage
          and give him a foxhound for company,

I will stand out front in a white linen suit
          surveying my plantation,

I will plant a magnolia tree.

But now, at the height of my visionary ecstasy,
          the telephone rings. It is the man
          next door, calling to let me know

that my sprinkler is turned up too high
and is sprinkling the seats of his convertible.

I go out to turn down the water, and I see
that the cedar needs trimming again,
that the elm twigs need to be raked.

I will do those things. I will hoe and trench
and weed, I will mow the grass.
I have moved in here now,

and I have to do what I can.

III *From Porlock*

The Writer-in-Residence Discusses His Working Habits

I often compose in my head
while working outside,
raking leaves or mowing the lawn
or feeding azaleas. Leaves
have sogged on my lawn
through two snows now.

———

I used to write with a fountain pen,
not typing until I had written
several longhand drafts.
But at my present level of fame
my books reach the galley-proof stage
without my having written a word.

———

Electricity furnishes
power for my lamp,
my cigarette lighter,
my pencil sharpener,
my typewriter,
and both of my tape recorders.

———

This piece of equipment
is a Veeder-Root counter.
It fits in the hand
like this, the thumb
poised on the button.
I count my words with it,
which requires concentration
since my rhythmical habit
is to count syllables.

———

I slip my wastepaper
into the basket
still flat,
in an upright stack.
If I crumple it,
it lies there uncrumpling
with a sound
between ticking and whispering.

————

The men in that photograph?
One is myself, somewhat
younger than I am now;
the other is Faulkner
or Stevens or Pound . . .
you can see from his expression
what good friends we were.

————

I have three calendars:
one above my desk
for decoration;
one in my pocket
for lectures and reading engagements;
and one in my filing cabinet
for the deaths of literary figures.

De Gustibus Ain't What Dey Used To Be

Poetry, like the old darky mowing the lawn, can't be hurried.

Marshall Fishwick

You have to know how to handle it.
Treated with understanding,
it is loyal, slow, and dependable,
with an earthy charm of its own.
　　　It walks into your life and sits down.

If it sometimes moves so sluggishly
that the grass grows up behind it
as fast as it's being cut,
you tell it to keep trying.
　　　It will not be hurried.

It shuffles and makes excuses
and tells you the mower is dull,
but you know better than that:
never trust it with machinery.
　　　It makes room for itself in your life.

It breaks everything it touches,
and steals what isn't nailed down;
its speech is a savage mumble,
and it lies just to keep in practice.
　　　There are things it will force you to see.

It promises to come back next week,
but you know it probably won't;
it is liable to get its throat cut
by another one just like it.
　　　It has settled on your life for good.

It shambles over the lawn
taking its own sweet time.
It can never be overworked;
it has a natural rhythm.
　　　It will stay. It will finally own you.

41

The New York Poet

So its the old lady mostly gets me down
these last few weeks
I mean a man has to take things easy
after a long day
stretch out
take off his shoes
watch some tv
                    maybe
drink a few beers evenins

& the old lady   what the hell
she know about it anyway
shes on my back
the minute she gets home
from the library
arms full of old paper bags
gum wrappers all thru her hair
she wants to know what the hell
I been doin   I tell her
I been tryin to keep body
& soul together   keep
her fat clothes on her fat ass

See them hands   shit
you dont think you get hands like that
on yr butt in front a tv
all the time   I work
like a sonofabitch all day
skin my knuckles tryin to straighten
secondhand frames   stringin
old wires across em   one thing & another
like to break my freakin back
hangin out 21st story windows the whole
damn day talkin to pilots & pigeons

I mean   a man has his work to do
but evenins   he wants to take
things easy
              jesus
just lookit them freakin hands

Every writer I know
hates other writers. Not all others, but most.
The ones who are better or different he has to hate
because they are better or different. And those who are worse
he despises because that is his earned right.

— *David R. Slavitt,*
The Eclogues of Virgil

Three Small
Seizures

INTERVIEW

"Why so pale and wan?"
  said Rod McKuen to Kahlil Gibran;
"Your graffiti have darkened my desperate ruin,"
  said Kahlil Gibran to Rod McKuen.

ON A POSTHUMOUS BOOK OF POEMS

These pages bring to mind, as I flip through
the efforts of the more-than-once-removed,
the poet's painful search for flawlessness:
what should not have survived an early purge
lies here as if it had the breath to bless
a hand that had no better work to do
than shuffling through a dead man's trash to forge
a corpus which a corpse might have improved.

TO AN OLDER POET

Young for my years, impertinent, perhaps
a poet and perhaps not — so you said.
I remind you, in a momentary lapse
of taste, that when I'm your age you'll be dead.

Pineapples
Since 1500

for Chippy Howe,
who, on a night
when she and all
her classmates
were hysterically
studying for a
history exam,
called me to
say that she could
not draw
pineapples.

Dates pass before my eyes, names,
dates, wars, discoveries, crowned heads,
and dates. They are not numbers
to me any more, but men and wars
and discoveries and names.
The wind howls at my window,
men march outside from down
the road, making war, discoveries,
dates. It is useless. I take up
my pen, my pad, attempt a bear
or two; too small and simple,
on the whole. A fruit or two —
a date — no, not a fruit like that.
A pineapple. Surmounted by
a crown of leaves, it sits, too round,
too crosshatched to be believed.
Another. Too tall and narrow; the edges
look like edges. Zig-zag? No.
The leaves don't look right, either.
An apple? A pine? Thin, red, tall,
green and round. Not so fat as that,
nameless kings and princes march
through my mind, ships on seas uncharted
sail to forgotten lands where perfect
pineapples await the sailors
as they steer their boats to shores
I can't remember, can't forget;
men march and halt and march in print
and leave me here with dreams of bears
among the ripe pineapples, though
the wind howls and time marches
in a double column, double time.

45

Another Message from Porlock

hark to the
musical clank

Walt Whitman

Toward Main Hall at the upper end of the quad,
as evening comes on, the literary gathering begins.
Going in, we can hear down the length of the veranda
the clatter of dinner dishes beginning to subside
in the kitchen. We trickle in to the Green Drawing Room,
browsing a moment among the few plush chairs reserved
for the handful of dignified regulars. Most of us
sit on the floor. Soon we take up the ritual signaling,
collecting in groups of friends who can make one ashtray
suffice, like a multiplied loaf. We settle down
for the introduction.
                              The poetry suits us. Here,
almost no one could seem far out of place; we welcome
what comes. Two poems to start, then a small joke;
we chuckle; we are friends. Growing deeper into himself,
he turns to his darker side, unraveling the energy
he builds toward his real platform pieces. Our breath
tightens; he carries us on a surf of words, on now
to his favorite, the long one we who are with him can follow.
Yet some of us glance at our watches, remembering
that even here a few things can arrive on schedule:

A sharp tap begins it; the listeners stiffen,
stop hearing the words of the poem. The ashtrays hang
in mid-pass: we all know what happens next.
Spang in the middle of a pivotal stanza,
the pipes in the walls fill with water and steam.
At first we try to ignore it, but none of us can:
we have been here before, and know what to expect.
Like a percolator picking up speed, the clamor
increases, and pauses, and then increases again
with a drunken battering, hissing, and thumping,
so that even the silences between pipeknocks have all
our attention, whether or not the poet proceeds.

46

Some of us wonder if we remember a pattern
in the way the banging climbs to a petulant stillness
that is filled, for a while, with our fears
that it probably will not last.
                              But it does,
and the poet is still reading on, having flinched
only once, more to acknowledge our embarrassment
than to register his. We settle again, and light up,
seeing silence redeemed by intrusion, silence
made ready at last to receive his hard-earned words.

To Hear
My Head
Roar

First, my father taught me to read poetry
aloud; then my teachers in grade school
remembered how he had recited poetry,

how many times he had brought down the school-
house with "Casey at the Bat." Whenever they
could they called me up before the whole school

to be my father's son. I still dream of days they
stood me shaking before my classmates, then
waited while I launched into what they

knew from long experience was coming, then
sat through "Jabberwocky" or "Excelsior" — that was
the full range of my repertoire by then.

Later I almost liked it, though I was
still forced to it: each week we all recited
at assembly. A terrible, tiring time that was

for my audience, and for me, as I recited
"The Highwayman" and "The Cremation of
Sam McGee." My father coached as I recited

nightly in the living room, and on the day of
my graduation from that place, my sister
and I recited, respectively, "The Ballad of

the Harp-Weaver" and "The Highwayman." My sister
and I fled to our father's side after
it was over, and I can still see my sister

blushing as the old ladies came up after
the performance with tears in their eyes
to tell my father we were wonderful. After

that, it was a long time before my eyes
would follow the tricks of poems, but now I know
dozens of them: they unscroll behind my eyes,

and I own hundreds of books in which I know
I can always find the right thing at the right time,
and I will read to anyone who doesn't know

what he is in for, for hours at a time.
When I try to understand this part of myself,
I think back to that earlier, troublesome time

to find that the explanation of myself
does not lie there entirely; for now I recall being
in high school, just beginning to take myself

seriously, and my father as a human being,
and I think of hours I spent in the attic
rummaging through old file cases, being

surprised to find, in the dark dust of that attic,
the poems my father had written when he
was in college. One afternoon in the attic

yielded an ancient treasure, a recording he
had once made and then forgotten. I
tiptoed out of the attic with it, thinking he

might take it from me, and secretly I
tried it, at first without success, on the machine
downstairs in the living room. At last I

even tried to start the reluctant machine
on the inner end of the groove. It worked.
The thing had been cut on some amateur's machine

and was made to run from the inside out. I worked
with the needle, nudging it over the cracks,
and heard, after what seemed hours of work,

a voice that I recognized, through dusty cracks
and thirty years, as my father's (or my own), say
something I now take to heart as my heart cracks:

"This is Tom Taylor talking; talking," I heard him say,
"to hear his own voice, and reading some poetry
  because he wants to have something to say."

IV *Harvest*

One side of his world is always missing.
You may give it a casual wave of the hand
or rub it with your shoulder as you pass,
but nothing on his blind side ever happens.

Riding a One-Eyed Horse

Hundreds of trees slip past him into darkness,
drifting into a hollow hemisphere
whose sounds you will have to try to explain.
Your legs will tell him not to be afraid

if you learn never to lie. Do not forget
to turn his head and let what comes come seen:
he will jump the fences he has to if you swing
toward them from the side that he can see

and hold his good eye straight. The heavy dark
will stay beside you always; let him learn
to lean against it. It will steady him
and see you safely through diminished fields.

Smoking in Bed in the Fire Chief's House

A gull drops clams on rocks
near where I lie taking what sun
there is above Nantucket, lulled almost
to sleep by the sound of waves, kept
awake by the thud of clams

on sand, and the rattling
sigh of salt-grass on the moors.
As the gull rises and falls, flickering in
and out of the corner of my eye,
the beach becomes the sheet

of my rented bed in town,
held as if by a ring of men. In a dull
daze between sleep and waking, I think the sheet
is slackened and pulled taut by hunters
in the north — they toss the gull,

the lightest hunter, high
into the air, so that from his perch
on nothing he can search for the blowhole
of the seal, the shifting whiteness
of the polar bear.

Closer to sleep, I become
the sharp-eyed hunter, tossed from the blanket
in time with waves; I rise above, then fall
below the gull, who hangs motionless
in the air beyond the rail

of the rolling ferry
that brought me here; he drifts
in and out of my field of vision as the boat
rocks slowly over the waves, lifting
me out of troughs, above

54

the waves, to look toward
the land I fled, as it recedes
into the distance beyond the stationary gull,
before I am caught, let down, then tossed
again to train my eyes

on the land beyond the shore,
to search out the quarry, whatever
it was I fled when I embarked. Driving
down the gangplank from the parking hold,
I carry glimpses of the world

I left behind — a face,
a cold flame around my heart, burning
images reduced to ash by time and distance:
glimpses that will fade, then blaze up,
as I drive to my rented room

in Irving Bartlett's house.
His wife shows me where things are; she points
at last to a brass gong above my bedroom door.
"It rings," she says, "whenever there's
a fire. My husband is

the Fire Chief here." So far,
it has clattered every day, only
to let the whole town know the noon hour
has arrived — there has been no alarm
set off by burning house

or tree, or by the flame
I cannot kindle in my brain.
Here nothing burns — not even my pale skin
in the slant sunlight. I pray
for sparks, but nothing catches fire

inside me or around me
as I ride the sounds of gulls and waves
to sleep, to dream myself astride a borrowed horse,
riding across the moors, listening
for gabbling beagles smoking

over a scent laid down
by hares. Beneath the horse's hooves
soft sand gives way along the beach where I lie
asleep, dreaming now of lying awake
with a lighted cigarette

in the Fire Chief's house,
thinking how the room might blaze around me
if I should fall asleep — how a fire might catch
hold of me once more, to wrap me
in tongues until my voice

could sing a name for the face
that chars within me. A *clack* beside
my head snaps me awake; I throw the broken
clam away, out over a rail that blurs
as sleep recedes toward

the shore I cannot see.
Awake at last, I watch this land
shine from the waves for the first time since I came.
The face I fled is ashes now,
and I can love the gull

who drops toward the clam
I threw out over moors where beagles
blaze over the trail of the hare, their voices
ringing in my ears, mingling with
the fire bell and the waves

until their flaming tongues
fill the air above the moors with song.
The face I wanted to name becomes this landscape,
named forever only by the sea.
My tongue on fire at last,

I rise from this beach,
turning toward the flame-touched song
of hounds. Under their smoking breath, in the wind,
the salt-grass burns on the sand
dunes, blade by blade.

Harvest

Every year in late July I come back to where I was raised,
to mosey and browse through old farm buildings,
over fields that seem never to change,

rummaging through a life I can no longer lead
and still cannot leave behind, looking for relics
which might spring back to that life at my touch.

Today, among thistles and ragweed, I stumble on
a discarded combine — the old kind we pulled
with a tractor to cut and thresh barley and wheat.

Now it lies listing into the side of this hill
like a stone or an uprooted stump, harboring snakes
and wasps, rusting slowly down into the briars.

Still, I climb to the seat, wondering whether it will
hold me, fumbling for pedals and levers
I used to know by heart. Above my head,

the grain-pipe forks down to the bag-clamps,
and a wad of tie-strings, gone weedy and rotten,
still hangs by my right hand. As I touch these things,

this machine I once knew by many unprintable names
moves out through barley in late July, and the stalks
fall to the knife as the paddle-reel sweeps them in.

On wide canvas belts, cut grain rides into the dark
insides of the combine, where frantic shakers and screens
break the grain loose from the stalks and the chaff;

almost invisible, small spines from the grain-heads
pour out through holes in the metal, billowing
into a cloud that moves with us over the hills,

58

engulfing me, the machine, the tractor and driver,
        as we work in a spiral to the center of the field,
        rolling back through the years in a dust cloud.

The spines stick to my skin, work into my pores,
        my bloodstream, and finally blaze into my head
        like a miniature cactus of hatred for all grain,

for flour and cereal and bread, for mildewed surplus
        swelling in midwestern silos. Never again,
        I thought once, as I rode out the cloud until sundown,

never again. I climb down and walk out through the thistles,
        still breathing fifteen-year-old barley. The years
        in the cloud drift back to me. Metal rusts into the hill.

Barley-dust pricks at my brain, and I am home.

San Francesco d'Assisi: Canticle of Created Things

Thine be the praise, good Lord
omnipotent, most high, Thine
the honor, the glory, and every blessing.
To Thee alone, most high, do these belong;
to speak Thy name no living man is worthy.

Be praised, my Lord, with all that Thou hast made;
above all else the sun, our master and our brother,
whence Thy gift of daylight comes.
He is most fair, and radiant with great splendor,
and from Thee, most high, his meaning comes.

Be praised, my Lord, for our sister moon,
        and for the stars;
Thou hast placed in the heavens their clear
        and precious beauty.
Be praised, my Lord, for our brother wind
and for the air, in all weathers cloudy and clear,
whence comes sustenance for all which Thou hast made.

Be praised, my Lord, for our sister water,
who is most useful, precious, humble and pure.

Be praised, my Lord, for our brother fire,
for Thine is the power by which he lights the dark;
Thine are his beauty and joy, his vigor and strength.

Be praised, my Lord, for earth, our mother
        and our sister;
by Thy power she sustains and governs us,
and puts forth fruit in great variety, with grass
        and colorful flowers.

Be praised, my Lord, for those who forgive
        by the power of Thy love within them,
for those who bear infirmities and trials;
blessed are those who endure in peace,
for Thou at last shalt crown them, O most high.

Be praised, my Lord, for our sister bodily death,
from whom no living man escapes;
woe unto those who die in mortal sin,
but blessed be those whom death shall find
        living by thy most sacred wishes,
for through the second death no harm
        shall come to them.

Praise my Lord and give thanks unto Him;
bless my Lord and humbly serve Him.

We watch him burn —
          hoof, hide, and bone.

                    — James Seay

Burning a Horse

Riding on a flatbed wagon, carrying with us
          an ax, pitchforks, a coil of heavy rope,
          and a five-gallon can of kerosene,

we went to the back meadow that afternoon,
          driven to desperate measures
          by the stench that hung on the still air,

dead air that lay like fog in the valley
          around us, not enough motion in it even
          to carry buzzards whose random glide

might have brought them to the body
          of the Percheron that festered on the grass
          where we had dragged him after he had died.

We spent an hour cutting brush from fallen trees,
          carrying it to where the horse lay bulging
          in the sun; we hooked him to the tractor

and pulled him over the pile of brush,
          to get it under him, then soaked
          the brushpile and his body with the kerosene.

I threw a match into the trembling vapors
          that rose from the fuel and from the rotting
          horse, then dropped back as the explosion

blasted us with the smell of burning hair. Slowly,
          one patch of skin, then another, burned through
          to let the gas escape and blaze like a blowtorch,

but the flames died down too soon, and we could hear
the flesh speaking, one of the men said, as
a cornfield does, growing after a hard rain.

We ran up to the pyre with more brush, holding
our breath as we used pitchforks to place
the dry sticks where they seemed needed most,

and then saw fire catch the wood, the flesh,
and saw black smoke so thick and heavy
that it hid us from each other; it crawled

down the meadow a few feet above the ground,
the smell we held our breath against
tainting everything it touched. Burning at last,

the horse was blackening and shrinking into the tall
meadow grass; and then, before us, there,
from coals that had caught hold in the horse's bones,

we saw a horse, made whole, with heavy flesh
and shining skin, rippling against the pull,
rising from the grass around the dying fire,

his new hoofs shod, his mane flying, rising
from the coals and moving in a smooth
and dangerous way; he traveled down the meadow

at a sweeping gallop, wrapped in something
like a flame, light and heat around him
that did not flicker or drop from him as he disappeared.

The sun rolled down the hill above the meadow,
and in the dusk a wind came up.
We strained our eyes, but the horse was gone,

moving perhaps beyond the stand of willow trees
at the upper end of the meadow, carrying
the light around him into darkness beyond our view.

We turned to look at the spot where the fire
had been, listening for the crackling
of smoldering bones, but all we heard

was our own blood and breath, and the sound
of the wind that must have carried him away. Ashes
lifted slowly in that wind, like heavy wings.

On a slope in deep woods below the dam,
I sat with a bird's voice cupped in my hands.
At my breath, a drumming chuckle rolled out
into the trees across the small ravine.

Again. I heard him answer back, and held
my breath, shifting to a crouch beside a tree,
moving one inch at a time to let the blood
flow tingling back into my deadened legs.

*Below
Carvin's
Cove*

for Clarice Short

Then between the leaves of a sumac bush
I saw his blue head move. I laid my cheek
against the stock and watched his colors change
the woods and touch the barrels of my gun.

Between us a narrow stream trickled on stone,
invisible under thirty feet of fog
that lined the bottom of the draw like smoke
poured out of a bottle. Its edges lapped
the trunks of oaks, and ghosts of chestnut trees
as white as bones stood rooted in that cloud.

The turkey drummed again; my finger tensed
too late: I saw him break into a run
straight down the hill toward me, leap to air,
then coast in a spiral downward, like a leaf,

free-falling toward the flowing cloud below,
skimming it, whipping up feathery wisps.
Downstream he sank for good. Above his wings
the fog heaved once and then lay still again.

I caught my breath and turned to look at leaves
that glowed where he had touched them with his wings;
my gun still pointed at the sumac bush
where I last saw him standing still. Far off,
I heard a voice like his, and cupped my hands.

65

My grandfather works in his garden today.
The death that grows inside him draws him there
to struggle with the death that takes away
the only thing he keeps against despair.

My Grandfather Works in His Garden

He sees me at the gate and comes to talk.
He leans against a post. His eyes go small
as he stares past me at a flower-stalk.
The years rise up between us like a wall.

I say it is too hot for him. He shifts
his weight toward me, but his eyes aim still
beyond me. Then they change: the barrier lifts,
disclosing shapes that I can only feel.

As his eyes change I am a boy once more,
and seem to see him straighten as one day
he straightened when a man came to our door
to tell him that our bull had got away,

that someone ought to go and bring him back.
I hear myself asking him not to go,
but as I speak I feel my voice fall slack,
reminding me that he already knew

the way love sometimes will not let you keep
a man from dangers that he knows are there.
I watch him now as he goes down the steep
porch steps and out the lane. For hours I stare

at where I saw him last. The window-glass,
when he returns, dissolves to let me break
from here to where the bull stands eating grass.
I watch the old man wave a stick and speak

to urge him up the lane, but when the bull
turns and stands like stone, I become one
with my grandfather, before a standing-still
I cannot see him try to face alone.

A hand grows tighter on the hickory cane.
The bull walks toward a man who seems at once
to stand inside behind a window pane
and out here in the path of that advance.

I stand alone. I raise my cane up high
and put my weight into swinging down
to stop the march of that unblinking eye.
Hickory snaps across a head of stone.

The head comes on until it strikes my chest
and I fall back between those heavy hooves
and close my eyes: now I am slowly pressed
into the ground as the great bull's weight moves

to his head. I feel my grandfather's breath
go slowly out of me. I brace my thumbs
for one inspired last move: I clench my teeth
against my whistling blood, my whole head hums —

my hands move upward toward the bull's round eyes.
I shove my thumbs in deep when I have found them,
and just before the bull begins to rise
I feel his eyelids closing tight around them.

My breath comes back with the window as the bull
gets to his feet and blindly moves away.
Until he is out of sight my grandfather lies still,
then rises slowly and slowly makes his way

toward me. I run out to meet him at the gate
he leans against. Green garden fills the space
rising behind him as he shifts his weight
and tells me it is hot. I touch his face.

was still, somewhere in her seventies, among
the last and toughest of the singlehanded
farmers in the country around our house.

In the wind, her long blue dress would ripple
and snap about her high-top shoes, as she rode
her hayrake hard behind her two black Percherons.

One day, years ago, we stood at the gate
and watched her working the field
half a mile away;

and when she saw us, she lifted the rake-teeth,
waved and yelled, whirled
the long black reins above her head,

and sent those heavy horses over the hills
toward us at a lumbering run — her blue sleeves

luffed like sails, the rake's steel wheels
touched the ground only once in a while.

At the gate, she gazed toward where she'd been,
and as she rolled her words
across the air between us,

Scotland's dark blue hills took shape upon those
fields where she worked alone to raise her beef,
to clear her hilly land of rocks.

"It does good where I pick them up," she said,
"and where I put them down."

Today, the last black Angus has been sold,
the last stray stone has found its place.

*Miss
Creighton*

Her Percherons, unharnessed now, walk side by side
      across the fields, toward what rose
      whenever she spoke:

they lean together for the last time into the pull,
      moving away from us
      over the dark blue hills of Scotland.

His name was
Mohammed Sceab

A descendant
of the emirs of the nomads
he killed himself
because he no longer had
a homeland

Giuseppe
Ungaretti:
In
Memoriam

He loved France
and changed his name

He became Marcel
but he was not French
and he forgot
how to live
in the tents of his people
where they listen to choruses
of the Koran
and sip coffee

And he forgot
how to set loose
the song
of his abandonment

I went with him
and the woman who owned the hotel
where we lived
in Paris
from number 5, rue des Carmes
a faded descending alley

He rests
in the graveyard at Ivry
a suburb which
always
seems like the last day
of a broken-down carnival

And perhaps I alone
still know
that he lived

Holding seminars at bay
with stern requirements and sly questioning
grows dull as days grow longer; spring
brings back an earlier time. Thoughts go astray.

An Old Rhodes Scholar

for Arthur Kyle Davis, Jr.

He finds himself gazing
beyond the aging trees outside his window
at a man his friends no longer know,
a strong-armed youth poised at the end of a blazing

playing field, stretching, warming
up, pacing off the runway, his tape-wound
bamboo pole beside him on the ground.
So long ago. He blinks to shake off swarming

visions that always return
to catch him napping: he lifts the vaulting pole
toward the bar, begins to roll
forward on his left foot to start his run.

Slowly the upper end
of the pole descends toward the mark
and he is raised in a sunlit arc
to the trembling bar. He hoists his feet, bends

his waist, then hangs, jack-
knife, above the sawdust pit for an instant
too perfect for the crowd of distant
admirers to believe, straightens his back,

then, like a cruising bird
that hunts for miles with hungry eyes to find
a furred or feathered something on the ground
and finally dives on widespread unheard

wings to earth, descends
to stand once more before these youthful faces.
    He fumbles with his notes, retraces
his steps, once more begins what never ends

    until those early days
return, unbidden, to interrupt a lecture
    on Wordsworth or the architecture
of an ode by Keats. Once more he turns away

    toward the window, pride
trembling in his voice as he recalls
    some old contest. The classroom falls
away to let us see him pausing, dignified,

    immaculate in tweeds,
his old-fashioned bamboo pole in his hands,
    ready to begin his run. He stands
a moment, thinking, then his right foot leads

    him toward the bar again,
while we, who have known him only in that room,
    are now amazed to see him in the bloom
of age, his paisley tie and gold stickpin

    flawlessly in place
as he picks up speed along the cinder runway,
    rises once more toward the bar, away
from rooms and lives he filled with ease and grace.

How Not To Domesticate Wildness might have been
the title for a course you never taught,
yet gave at every turn, with every breath
taking to heart the mind's life among ferns,
moles, birds, wild humans and Anglophile dogs.

*For Julia
Randall*

*on her retirement
from Hollins
College, 1973*

I hear you say, *You make things with their names,
but all these names are what get in the way.*
What's the right word for how you leave us, then?
How shall I name a pleasurable regret?
I say the view changes, as you said it would.

Whenever I try to follow you out to the edges
of everything, hunting the words for praise,
I will find my way by stones that you have named.

*Return to
the Old
Friends*

This Meeting House, rising from a rejoicing
April landscape, is emptied of all music,
though sunlight glances brightly from the crimson
flowers by the road. We feel the hollow clash
of mystery in this liveliness, opposing
the final smallness of our hopes that peace

may be with him forever, whose life was peace.
My grandfather is here, beyond all the rejoicing
he carried into his legendary garden, opposing
the encroachment of things he had not planted, music
rising from around him in those days as the clash
of hoe on stone struck sparks of crimson

until the whole garden seemed stained crimson
with his foes' blood. Yet, by his labor, peace
flourished in his garden, until, as at a clash
of cymbals, we find him, far from all rejoicing;
we walk to our seats as to a solemn music.
Years have gone by since I left here, opposing

all that this house gave me while opposing
mysteries called me to other places, crimson
pageantries these Friends distrust. What music
did I look for when I left this house of peace,
shaking certain hands for the last time, rejoicing
in what I thought my victory in the old clash

with all that fathered me? I relive that clash,
trying to recall the force I was opposing
in my father's calm eyes as I fled rejoicing.
Now it is Easter, spring is green and crimson,
yet his father lies here. I come in peace
to greet old Friends once more, in search of music

that deserted me at my departure, music
free of pageantry or sound, without the clash
of bells that signal anything but peace.
My grandfather lies still as stone, opposing
my wish for breath below the touch of crimson,
yet in his presence now I stand rejoicing.

This silent music in my blood, opposing
the clash of sunlight dancing on crimson,
leads me toward peace and a strange rejoicing.

Bernard and Sarah

"Hang them where they'll do some good," my grandfather
said, as he placed the dusty photograph
in my father's hands. My father and I stared
at two old people posed stiffly side by side —
my great-great-great-grandparents, in the days
when photography was young, and they were not.
My father thought it out as we drove home.

Deciding that they might do the most good
somewhere out of sight, my father drove
a nail into the back wall of his closet;
they have hung there ever since, brought out
only on such occasions as the marriage
of one of his own children. "I think you ought
to know the stock you're joining with," he says.

Then back they go to the closet, where they hang
keeping their counsel until it is called for.
Yet, through walls, over miles of fields and woods
that flourish still around the farm they cleared,
their eyes light up the closet of my brain
to draw me toward the place I started from,
and when I have come home, they take me in.

An Afternoon of Pocket Billiards was set in Intertype Baskerville
with handset Baskerville Foundry display type,
printed by the University of Utah Printing Service
on Warren's Olde Style Wove
with Strathmore Americana Text end papers,
and bound in Columbia's Fictionette
by Mountain States Bindery.

Typography by Donald M. Henriksen.

Design by Bailey-Montague & Associates.